Power Maths

Year 2 Textbo

C000008811

Series Editor: Tony Staneff

Flo
Flo is flexible.
She looks for
different
ways to solve
a problem.

curious

brave

determined

helpful

Ash

Astrid

Dexter

Sparks

P **Pearson**

Contents

This shows us what page to turn to.

I cannot wait to learn these new things!

How to use this book

Do you remember how to use Power Maths?

These pages help us get ready for a new unit.

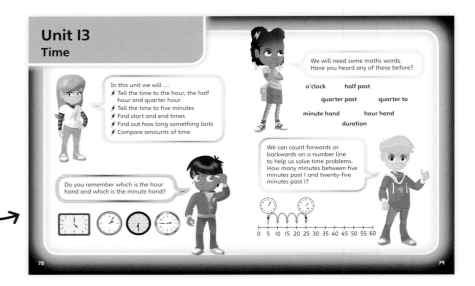

Discover

Lessons start with Discover.

Have fun exploring new maths problems.

Share

Next, we share what we found out.

Did we all solve the problems the same way?

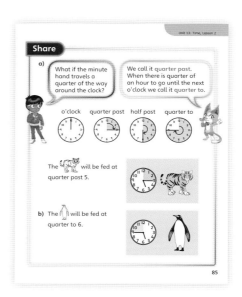

Think together

Then we have a go at some more problems together.

We will try a challenge too!

This tells you which page to go to in your Practice Book.

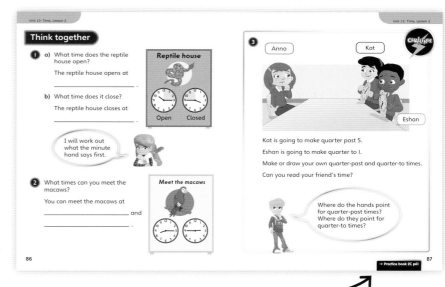

At the end of a unit we will show how much we can do!

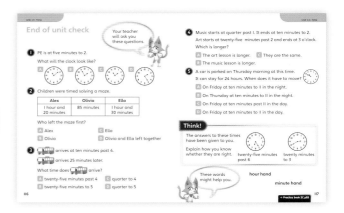

Unit 11
Position and direction

In this unit we will ...
- ⚡ Describe movement
- ⚡ Describe turns
- ⚡ Make patterns by turning shapes

We will use shapes to make patterns. Can you say which shape has made a half turn?

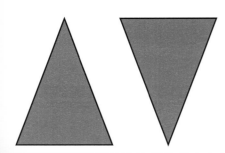

We will need some maths words. Which of these are new?

clockwise   **anticlockwise**   **forwards**

backwards   **left**   **right**   **middle**

turn   **half turn**   **quarter turn**

three-quarter turn

Do you think this is a clockwise or an anticlockwise turn?

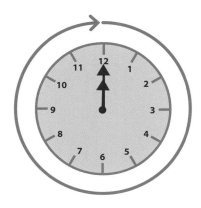

Describing movement

Discover

1 **a)** Follow the instructions on the screen to complete the dance.

b) Describe the movements in the dance.

Share

a) and **b)** These are the movements in the dance.

 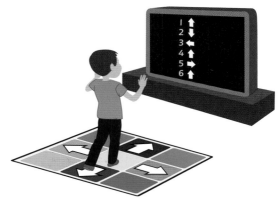

Step 1: forwards

Step 2: backwards

Step 3: left

Step 4: forwards

 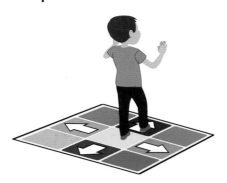

Step 5: right

Step 6: forwards

I know to use forwards, backwards, left and right to describe movement.

Think together

1 Here are three sandcastles.

Complete the sentences.

The _____ flag is in the middle.

The green spotty flag is to the left of the _____ flag.

The _____ flag is to the right of the green spotty flag.

2

a) To move from the ♥ to the ☀, move ☐ square up and ☐ square left.

b) Describe how to move from the ★ to the ☀.

Can you do this in more than one way?

3 Jake the mouse is in one of the squares in the field.

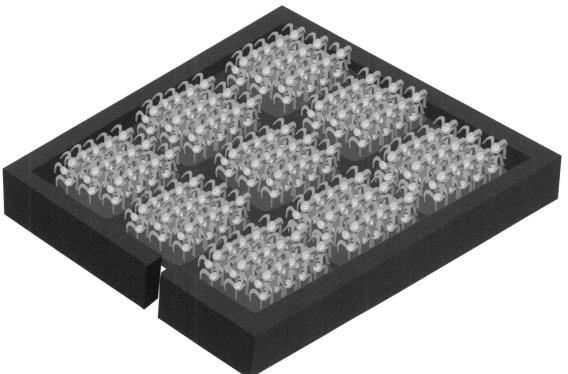

Jake moves away from the entrance:

1 square forwards

1 square left

1 square backwards

1 square right.

Where does Jake finish?

I wonder where Jake could have started.

11

→ Practice book 2C p6

Describing turns

Discover

1 **a)** Sam is facing the 🐐 .

She makes a half turn.

What is Sam facing now?

b) Sam faces the 🐄 .

She makes a quarter turn left.

What is she facing now?

Share

a)

Sam is facing the now.

b)

Sam turned left.
This is **anticlockwise**.

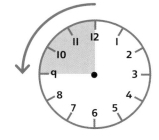

If Sam turned right, this would be **clockwise**.

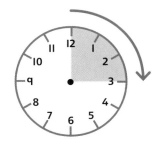

Sam is facing the now.

Think together

1 Choose clockwise or anticlockwise to describe how Sam turns.

a) 🐐 to 🐓 is a quarter turn

_____ .

b) 🐴 to 🐄 is a three-quarter

turn _____ .

c) 🐓 to 🐓 is a whole turn

_____ .

I wonder if there is more than one answer for the last sentence.

2 Match each picture to the correct description.

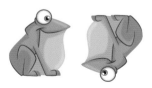

Three-quarter turn clockwise

Quarter turn clockwise

Half turn anticlockwise

3

 to is a quarter turn anticlockwise.

 to is a three-quarter turn clockwise.

 to is two quarter turns clockwise.

 Harry

 Amelia

Dai

Who is correct? Explain why.

 Can more than one sentence be correct if they are described differently?

15

→ Practice book 2C p9

Describing movement and turns

Discover

1 **a)** Help the  reach the treasure safely.

Write instructions to get him to the treasure.

Use these words: forwards, backwards, clockwise, anticlockwise, quarter turn.

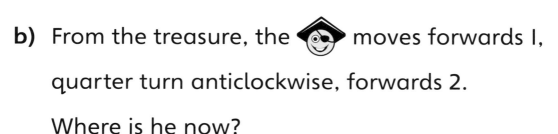

b) From the treasure, the  moves forwards 1, quarter turn anticlockwise, forwards 2.

Where is he now?

Share

a) To get the treasure, the needs to move

forwards 2

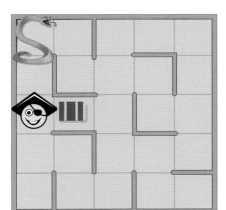

quarter turn
clockwise

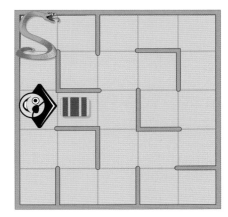

forwards 1

b)

forwards 1

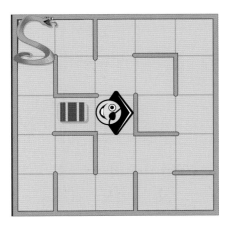

quarter turn
anticlockwise

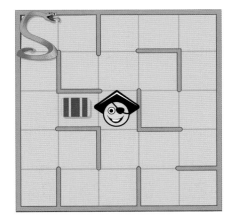

forwards 2

Think together

 1

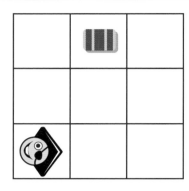

Put the sentences in the correct order to show how the can get to the treasure chest. Use 1st, 2nd, 3rd.

Go forwards 2 spaces ⬜

Make a quarter turn anticlockwise ⬜

Go forwards 1 space ⬜

2

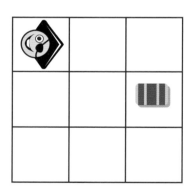

Complete the sentences to describe how the pirate can get to the treasure chest.

Go _____ ⬜ spaces.

Make a _____ turn _____ .

Go _____ ⬜ space.

18

③

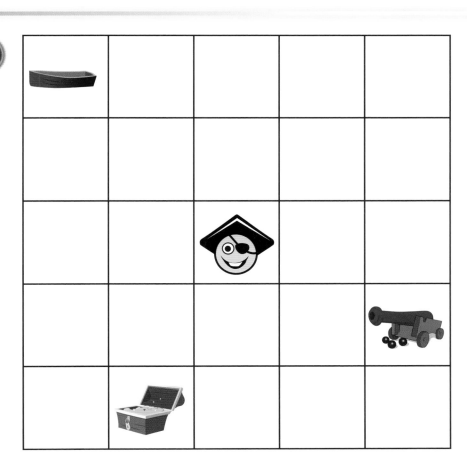

If the  follows the instructions, where will he be?

1 step forwards

Quarter turn anticlockwise

2 steps forwards

Three-quarter turn anticlockwise

1 step forwards

Can you make up your own story to get to a different place?

19

Making patterns with shapes

Discover

I **a)** What will the next two shapes in the pattern look like?

b) What is the same about the shapes in the pattern?

What is different?

Share

a) The next two shapes will be

b) All the shapes are triangles.

They all have three sides.

They are all the same size and colour.

The triangles are in a different position. They have made a half turn after each shape in the pattern.

The first 3 sentences are what are the same about these shapes.

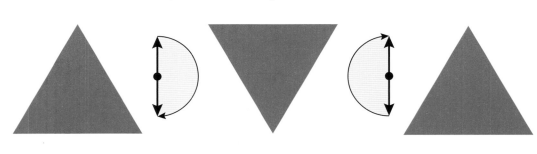

I wonder if the triangle has turned clockwise or anticlockwise.

Think together

1 **a)** Tick the shape that comes next in the pattern.

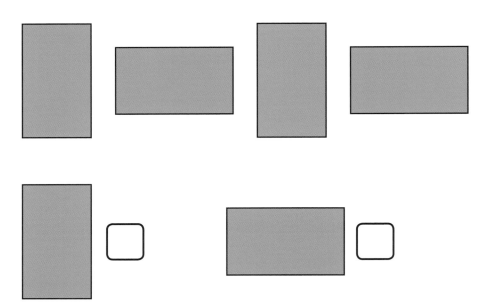

b) Describe the turn it makes.

The ▮ makes a _____ turn each time.

2 Describe the missing shape.

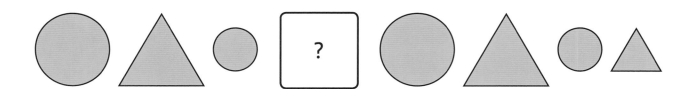

A _____ is missing.

3 What will the next three shapes in the pattern be?

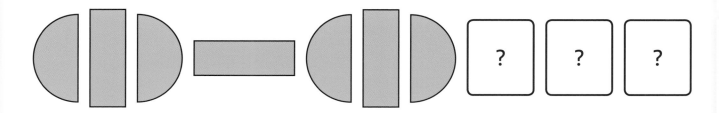

I wonder how I can describe the pattern.

Make your own repeating pattern. Challenge your friend.

23

→ Practice book 2C p15

End of unit check

Your teacher will ask you these questions.

1 Which sentence **does not** describe the turn?

A Quarter turn clockwise

B Three-quarter turn anticlockwise

C Quarter turn anticlockwise

D Quarter turn right

2 Which instructions will get the man to the 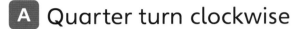?

A Forwards 3, quarter turn anticlockwise, forwards 1

B Forwards 3, quarter turn clockwise, forwards 1

C Forwards 3, quarter turn left, forwards 1

D Quarter turn right, forwards 1, quarter turn left, forwards 2

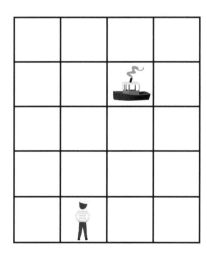

3 Describe how the heart shape turns.

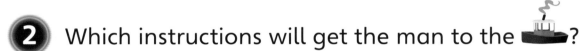

A Half turn

C Whole turn

B Quarter turn anticlockwise

D Quarter turn clockwise

4 Which image completes the pattern?

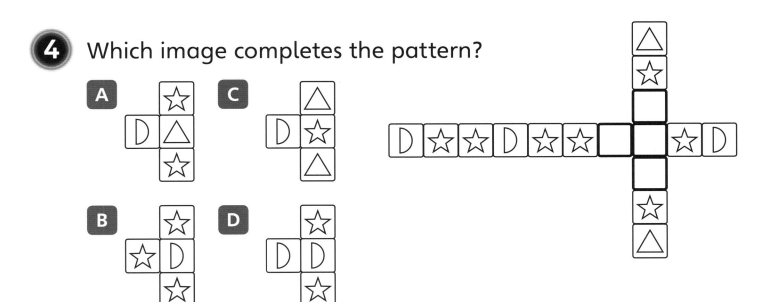

A

B

C

D

Think!

Ask your partner to choose an item.

Write out questions you could ask to work out which item they have chosen.

For example: Is it on the top row?

These words might help you.

left

above

top

right

below

bottom

25

Unit 12
Problem solving and efficient methods

In this unit we will …
- ⚡ Compare ways of calculating
- ⚡ Use mental addition and subtraction
- ⚡ Look for the most efficient way to solve a problem
- ⚡ Use number facts to solve problems
- ⚡ Solve word problems using all four operations

1	2	3	4	5	6	7	8	9	10
11	12	13	14	15	16	17	18	19	20
21	22	23	24	25	26	27	28	29	30
31	32	33	34	35	36	37	38	39	40
41	42	43	44	45	46	47	48	49	50
51	52	53	54	55	56	57	58	59	60
61	62	63	64	65	66	67	68	69	70
71	72	73	74	75	76	77	78	79	80
81	82	83	84	85	86	87	88	89	90
91	92	93	94	95	96	97	98	99	100

We will use a 100 square to help us. What is 22 more than 46?

26

We will need some maths words. Have you heard any of these before?

number facts **calculate mentally**

bar model **number line**

part-whole model **100 square**

We can use a bar model to help us add, subtract, multiply and divide. Can you use this bar model to calculate 17 + ☐ = 40?

40	
17	?

My way, your way!

Discover

1 **a)** How much will it cost in total to post the letter and the parcel?

b) How much change will there be from a £1 coin?

Share

I will use the bar model to find out what the problem is.

a)

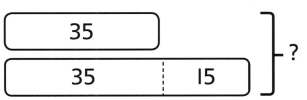

letter | 35
parcel | 35 | 15
?

Letter: 35p

Parcel: 35p + 15p = 50p

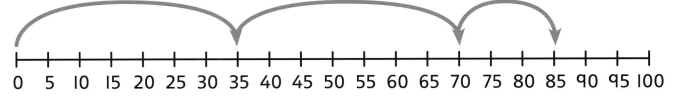

```
0  5  10  15  20  25  30  35  40  45  50  55  60  65  70  75  80  85  90  95  100
```

```
  T  O            T  O
  3  5            5  0
+ 1  5          + 3  5
  5  0            8  5
     1
```

It will cost 85p to post the letter and the parcel.

b) There are 100 pence in £1.

100p

| 35p | 50p | ? |
| letter | parcel | change |

To find the change from £1, work out the difference between 85p and 100p (£1).

85p + 15p = 100p

100p − 85p = 15p

There will be 15p change from a £1 coin.

Think together

 Sam wants to post two cards using next day delivery.

He has £1.

Does he have enough money?

Price list for posting a card	
Normal delivery	35p
Next day delivery	45p
Signed for	Extra 20p

?

45p	45p

45 + 45 = ☐

The total cost is ☐ p.

Sam does/does not have enough money because

_____ .

2 Sam sends two cards using normal delivery.

How much change will he get from £1?

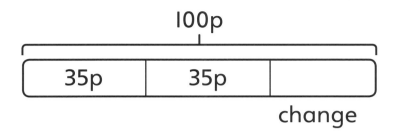

$\boxed{} + \boxed{} = \boxed{}$

$100p - \boxed{}p = \boxed{}$

Sam will get $\boxed{}$ change.

3 Sam sends one card to be signed for the next day.

CHALLENGE

He sends the other card with normal post.

He has £1. Is that enough money?

card 1

card 2

Sam _____ enough money.

→ **Practice book 2C p20**

Using number facts

Discover

1 a) To help him solve $15 + 8 = \boxed{}$, Arun started by

doing $5 + 8 = 13$. Explain his strategy.

b) Use the same strategy to solve these:

$25 + 8 = \boxed{}$

$35 + 8 = \boxed{}$

$8 + 45 = \boxed{}$

Share

I wonder how 15 + 8 is related to 5 + 8.

I will use the sum of 5 + 8 to find 15 + 8 without calculating from the beginning again.

a)

5 + 8 = 13

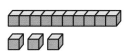

15 is 10 more than 5.

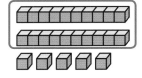

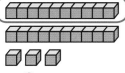

15 + 8 must be 10 more than 5 + 8.

15 + 8 = 23

Arun added the 1s first, then added the 10.

b) 25 + 8

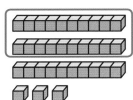

25 + 8 = 33

35 + 8

35 + 8 = 43

8 + 45

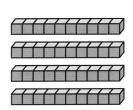
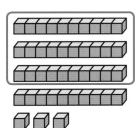

8 + 45 = 53

Think together

 1

$$59 + 6 = 65$$

Use this calculation to work out:

a) 79 + 6

79 is ☐ more than 59.

Therefore 79 + 6 = ☐.

b) 29 + 6

29 is ☐ less than 59.

Therefore 29 + 6 = ☐.

2

$$24 + 37 = 61$$

Use this calculation to work out 24 + 67.

☐ is ☐ more than ☐.

Therefore 24 + 67 = ☐.

3

$$28 + 36 =$$

$28 + 36 = \boxed{}$

Find the answer.

How could you use it to help these children work out their answers?

I need to work out 76 + 28.

I need to work out 38 + 26.

I wonder how much greater or smaller each answer is.

I think two of the questions might have the same answer.

35

Using number facts and equivalence

Discover

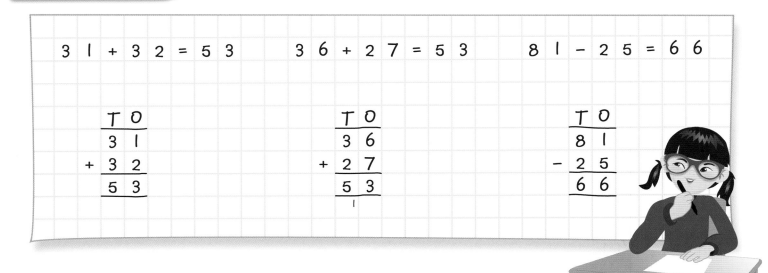

1 a) What error has been made in the first question?

b) Are these correct? Explain your thinking.

$$36 + 27 = 53 \qquad 81 - 25 = 66$$

	T	O
	3	6
+	2	7
	5	3

	T	O
	8	1
−	2	5
	6	6

Share

a)

I will start by using a fact that I know.

I do not need to calculate the total to find out if the total is correct.

You know that 30 + 30 = 60, so the sum of 31 and 32 must be more than 60, which means 53 is incorrect.

The correct answer is 31 + 32 = 63.

The 10s have been added incorrectly.

```
  T O
  3 1
+ 3 2
  6 3
```

b) 30 + 20 = 50, but 6 + 7 is more than 3, so 53 must be incorrect.

The correct answer is 36 + 27 = 63.

```
  T O
  3 6
+ 2 7
  6 3
  1
```

81 − 20 = 61, which is less than 66. There is also another 5 to subtract, so 66 must be incorrect.

The correct answer is 81 − 25 = 56.

```
  T O
  7̶8̶ ¹1
−   2 5
    5 6
```

Think together

1 Is this calculation correct?

If not, correct it and explain your thinking.

```
5 4 + 1 8 = 6 2

    T O
    5 4
  + 1 8
    6¹ 2
```

First I will add the 1s.

2 Is this calculation correct?

If not, correct it and explain your thinking.

```
3 + 5 6 = 8 6

    T O
    3
  + 5 6
    8 6
```

I wonder if 56 + 3 will be as much as 86.

Do I even need to set this out in columns?

3 Is this calculation correct?

If not, correct it and explain your thinking.

$$43 - 4 = 41$$

T	O
4	3
−	4
4	1

I know 3 is less than 4.
I think I need to exchange
1 ten for 10 ones.

→ Practice book 2C p26

Using a 100 square

Discover

1 **a)** What is 8 more than 45? How can you use the 100 square for support?

b) What is 32 more than 45? How can you use the 100 square for support?

Share

a)

I am going to count on using the 100 square.

Remember, there are ten squares in every row.

Count on 8 from 45.

46, 47, 48, 49, 50, 51, 52, 53

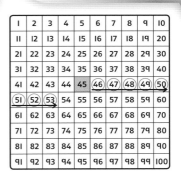

Or count on 10 by moving down to the next row. Then count back 2, because 10 is 2 more than 8.

45, 55, 54, 53

So, the answer is 45 + 8 = 53.

b) Count on in 1s from 45.

46, 47, 48, 49, 50, 51 77

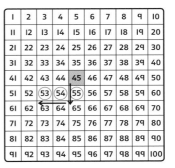

Or count on in 10s from 45. Then count on in 1s from 75.

55, 65, 75, 76, 77

So the answer is 45 + 32 = 77.

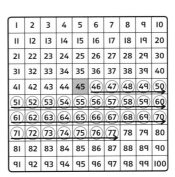

41

Think together

1 What is 36 more than 52?

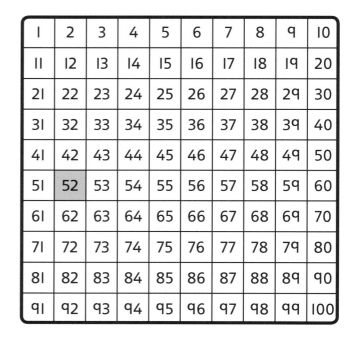

1	2	3	4	5	6	7	8	9	10
11	12	13	14	15	16	17	18	19	20
21	22	23	24	25	26	27	28	29	30
31	32	33	34	35	36	37	38	39	40
41	42	43	44	45	46	47	48	49	50
51	52	53	54	55	56	57	58	59	60
61	62	63	64	65	66	67	68	69	70
71	72	73	74	75	76	77	78	79	80
81	82	83	84	85	86	87	88	89	90
91	92	93	94	95	96	97	98	99	100

36 more than 52 is ☐.

2 What is 45 less than 76?

1	2	3	4	5	6	7	8	9	10
11	12	13	14	15	16	17	18	19	20
21	22	23	24	25	26	27	28	29	30
31	32	33	34	35	36	37	38	39	40
41	42	43	44	45	46	47	48	49	50
51	52	53	54	55	56	57	58	59	60
61	62	63	64	65	66	67	68	69	70
71	72	73	74	75	76	77	78	79	80
81	82	83	84	85	86	87	88	89	90
91	92	93	94	95	96	97	98	99	100

45 less than 76 is ☐.

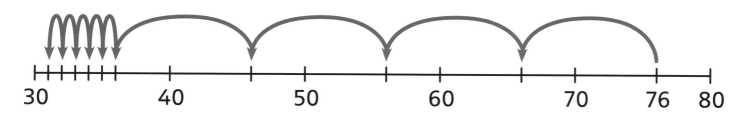

3 Millie is working out 68 − 26 on a 100 square.

1	2	3	4	5	6	7	8	9	10
11	12	13	14	15	16	17	18	19	20
21	22	23	24	25	26	27	28	29	30
31	32	33	34	35	36	37	38	39	40
41	42	43	44	45	46	47	48	49	50
51	52	53	54	55	56	57	58	59	60
61	62	63	64	65	66	67	68	69	70
71	72	73	74	75	76	77	78	79	80
81	82	83	84	85	86	87	88	89	90
91	92	93	94	95	96	97	98	99	100

Show Millie's calculation on a number line.

40   50   60   68 70

→ Practice book 2C p29

Getting started

Discover

Filip: The sum of my cards is 14.

Kat: My cards also add up to 14.

1 a) Each child has a set of number cards from 1 to 9.
   Which two cards could Filip have?

   ☐ + ☐ = 14

b) One of Kat's numbers is the same as Filip's. Which three cards could Kat have?

   ☐ + ☐ + ☐ = 14

Share

a)

I will pick one card first, then look for the other one.

I am going to see how many more I need to make 14.

2

If Filip picks up 2: $14 - 2 = 12$

There is no card for 12, the biggest number is 9.

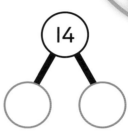

9

If Filip picks up 9: $14 - 9 = 5$

There is a card for 5.

$9 + 5 = 14$

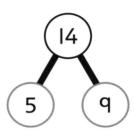

Filip could have the cards 9 and 5.

b) $9 + 5 = 14$

Partition 9 or 5 to find three numbers which total 14.

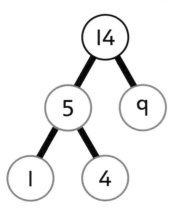

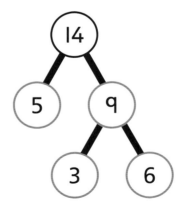

$1 + 4 + 9 = 14$ $5 + 3 + 6 = 14$

Kat could have the cards 1, 9 and 4. Or she could have the cards 5, 3 and 6.

Think together

1 Find all the pairs of cards that add up to 14.

| 1 | 2 | 3 | 4 | 5 | 6 | 7 | 8 | 9 |

Use a part-whole model to help you.

☐ + ☐ = 14

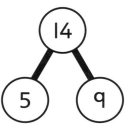

I wonder why 13 and 12 are crossed out.

First card	1	2	3	4	5	6	7	8	9
Second card	1̶3̶	1̶2̶			9				

2 Find two more sets of three numbers which add up to 14.

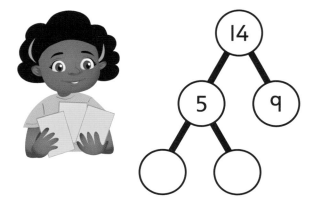

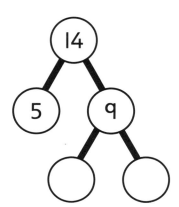

I wonder if it is possible to find them all.

46

3 Both children make 14 using only one set of numbers, 1 to 9, shared between them.

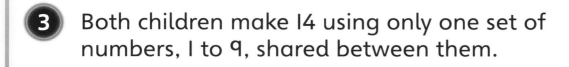

What could their numbers be?

Use what you found out in question 1.

I think this means you cannot have more than one of the same number.

47

→ Practice book 2C p32

Missing numbers

Discover

1 **a)** How much money did Marta have before her father gave her £20?

£55 = £20 + ☐

b) Marta wants to donate £100 to a charity that protects birds. How much more does she need to save?

£55 + ☐ = £100

Share

a)

I know one part is 20 and the whole is 55. I need to work out the missing part.

To find a part I can do a subtraction: 55 – 20 = ?

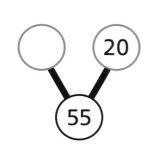

I can draw or use 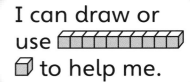 to help me.

55

| 35 | 20 |

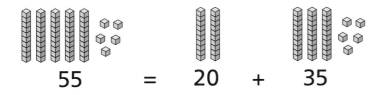

55 = 20 + 35

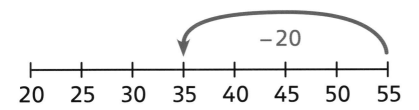

55 = 20 + 35

Marta had £35 before her father gave her £20.

49

b)

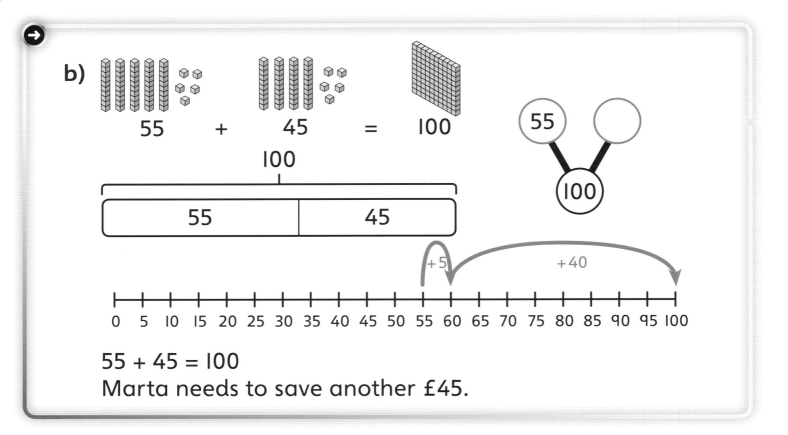

55 + 45 = 100
Marta needs to save another £45.

Think together

1 A box holds 40 cups. There are 18 cups on the table.
How many more cups are needed to fill the box?

$18 + \boxed{} = 40$

$40 - 18 = \boxed{}$

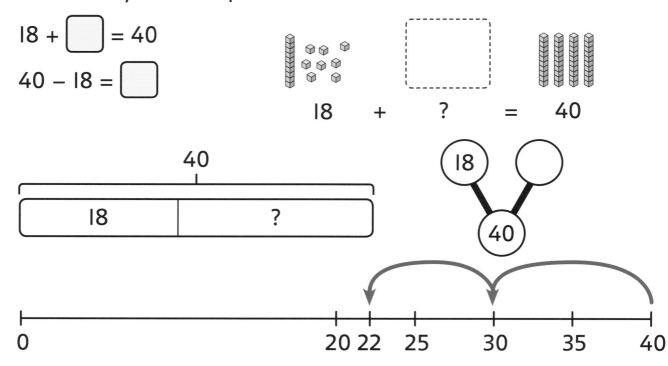

50

2 A muffin costs 68p. Joe has 38p.

How much more does he need to buy a muffin?

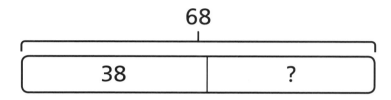

⬜ + ⬜ = ⬜

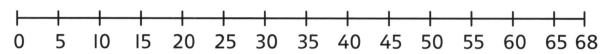

+ ? =

68

| 38 | ? |

68

0 5 10 15 20 25 30 35 40 45 50 55 60 65 68

3 Find the value of ✦ and complete the series of calculations.

CHALLENGE

22 + ✦ = 56

⬜ + ✦ = 57

⬜ + ✦ = 58

⬜ + ✦ = 59

⬜ + ✦ = 60

I can use one fact to find many more.

51

Mental addition and subtraction ❶

Discover

I am 31 years older than you.

You are 61 years younger than me.

I am 11 years older than you.

Today is my birthday.

Tim

❶ **a)** How old is Tim's brother?

b) How old is Tim's mum?

Share

a)

I will use column addition.

I do not need to use column addition. I can **calculate mentally**!

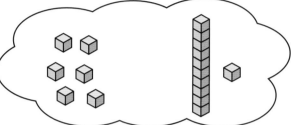

Add the 1s.

6 + 1 = 7 so

6 + 11 = 17

Tim's brother is 17 years old.

b) 6 + 31 = 37

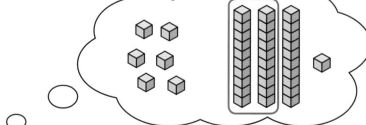

31 is 20 more than 11, so just add 20 to Tim's brother's age.

17 + 20 = 37

Tim's mum is 37 years old.

I can see that 6 + a 2-digit number ending in 1 will always be a 2-digit number ending in 7.

Think together

1 How old is Tim's grandma?

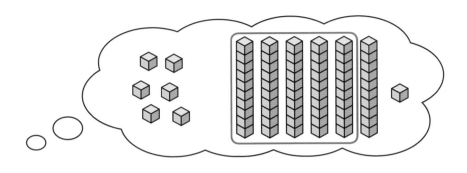

6 + 6I = ☐

Tim's grandma is ☐ years old.

What pattern can you see?

2 Tim's mum is 37 years old.

Tim's grandpa is 40 years older than Tim's mum.

How old is Tim's grandpa?

☐ + ☐ = ☐

Show how you found this out in two different ways.

3

There are different ways I can work out calculations in my head.

Look at these calculations.

Which ones can you do in your head?

25 + 4 = ☐   25 – 4 = ☐

42 + 30 = ☐   42 – 30 = ☐

36 + 7 = ☐   36 – 7 = ☐

28 + 12 = ☐   38 – 18 = ☐

Explain to your teacher how you did them mentally.

I will draw what is going on in my mind.

→ Practice book 2C p38

Mental addition and subtraction ❷

Discover

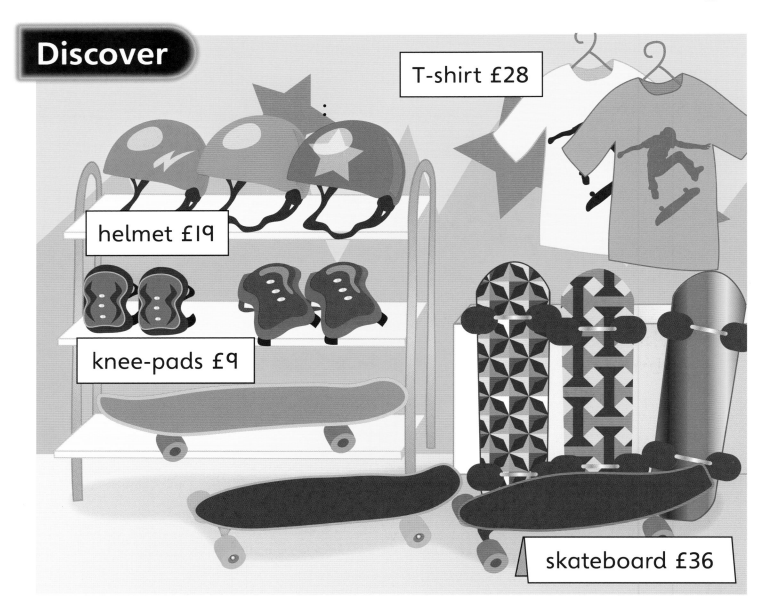

T-shirt £28

helmet £19

knee-pads £9

skateboard £36

❶ **a)** How much does a skateboard and a pair of knee-pads cost?

b) Gary buys a different skateboard and a helmet.

The total cost is £56.

How much does his skateboard cost?

Share

a) 36 + 9 = ⬜

> I can count on 9.

Count on in 1s: 36 + 9 = 45

> You can add too much and take away the extra.

1	2	3	4	5	6	7	8	9	10
11	12	13	14	15	16	17	18	19	20
21	22	23	24	25	26	27	28	29	30
31	32	33	34	35	36	37	38	39	40
41	42	43	44	45	46	47	48	49	50
51	52	53	54	55	56	57	58	59	60
61	62	63	64	65	66	67	68	69	70
71	72	73	74	75	76	77	78	79	80
81	82	83	84	85	86	87	88	89	90
91	92	93	94	95	96	97	98	99	100

9 is one less than 10. Add 10 (which is one too many), then subtract 1.

36 + 9 = 36 + 10 − 1 = 45

£36 + £9 = £45

A skateboard and a pair of knee-pads cost £45.

1	2	3	4	5	6	7	8	9	10
11	12	13	14	15	16	17	18	19	20
21	22	23	24	25	26	27	28	29	30
31	32	33	34	35	36	37	38	39	40
41	42	43	44	45	46	47	48	49	50
51	52	53	54	55	56	57	58	59	60
61	62	63	64	65	66	67	68	69	70
71	72	73	74	75	76	77	78	79	80
81	82	83	84	85	86	87	88	89	90
91	92	93	94	95	96	97	98	99	100

b) 56 − 19 = ⬜

> You can subtract more and then add the extra.

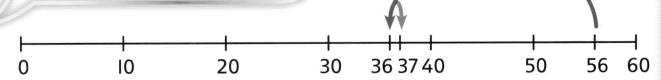

56 − 19 = 56 − 20 + 1 = 37

Gary's skateboard costs £37.

Think together

1 How much do a pair of roller blades at £54 and a helmet at £19 cost altogether?

1	2	3	4	5	6	7	8	9	10
11	12	13	14	15	16	17	18	19	20
21	22	23	24	25	26	27	28	29	30
31	32	33	34	35	36	37	38	39	40
41	42	43	44	45	46	47	48	49	50
51	52	53	54	55	56	57	58	59	60
61	62	63	64	65	66	67	68	69	70
71	72	73	74	75	76	77	78	79	80
81	82	83	84	85	86	87	88	89	90
91	92	93	94	95	96	97	98	99	100

$54 + 19 = \boxed{}$

$54 + 20 - \boxed{} = \boxed{}$

The total cost is £$\boxed{}$.

2 T-shirts are on sale. They cost £29 for two.

How much change will Lois get from £50?

$50 - 29 = \boxed{}$

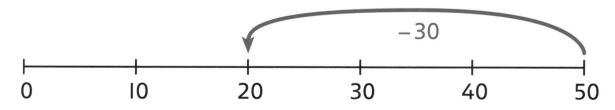

$50 - 29 = 50 - \boxed{} + \boxed{} = \boxed{}$

Lois will get £$\boxed{}$ change.

3 Kara and Shaan are working out calculations in their heads.

What calculation are they each trying to work out?

56 − ☐ = ☐

> I will subtract 30 and then add on 1.

Kara

37 + ☐ = ☐

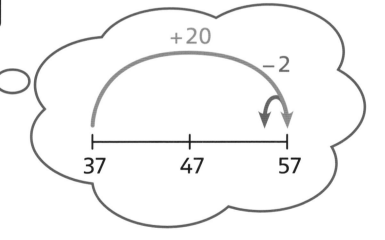

+20

−2

37   47   57

Shaan

> I wonder if a number line will help me to see what is going on.

→ **Practice book 2C p41**

Efficient subtraction

Discover

1 **a)** What is the missing number?

$$\triangle - \bigcirc = \square$$

b) What is the missing number?

$$\triangle - \blacksquare = \square$$

Share

a) Draw 61 circles and cross out 18 of them.

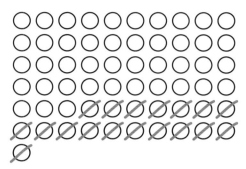

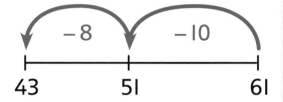
I can subtract one by one.

Use a number line to take away 10 and then take away 8.

$61 - 18 = 43$

The missing number is 43.

You could also use a 100 square.

b) Crossing out 56 circles takes too long.

Use a number line. First take away 50 and then take away 6.

$61 - 56 = 5$

The missing number is 5.

I know that $61 - 56 = 5$ and $56 + 5 = 61$ are the same.

I can count on 5 instead.

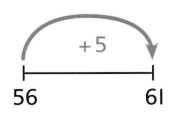

Think together

1 $\blacksquare - \bigcirc = \square$

■ = 56

▲ = 61

● = 18

Choose your own method to solve this.

$\square - \square = \square$

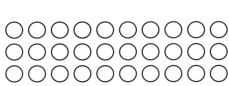

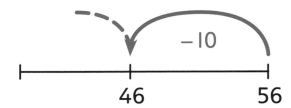

−10

46   56

2 Write the answers.

What do you notice about the answers?

$\blacksquare - 49 = \square$ $\blacksquare - 47 = \square$

$\blacksquare - 48 = \square$ $\blacksquare - 46 = \square$

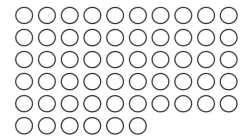

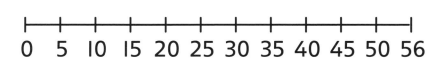

0   5   10   15   20   25   30   35   40   45   50   56

I think it might be easier to count on than take away.

3 △ = 81　　　　　　　◯ = 72

　　■ = 8　　　　　　　☆ = 48

△ − ◯ = ▢

☆ − ■ = ▢

△ − ■ = ▢

◯ − ▢ = ☆

What different methods would you use to solve these?

Discuss with your partner which methods you think suit the problems best.

Do they agree?

→ **Practice book 2C p44**

Solving problems – addition and subtraction

Cup of tea: 40p

Teacake: 58p

Egg:

Toast:

1 **a)** How much does a cup of tea and a teacake cost altogether?

b) 🍳 + 🍞 = 74p.

🍳 + 🍳 + 🍞 = £1.

How much does one piece of toast cost?

Share

a) A cup of tea costs 40p.

A teacake costs 58p.

$40p + 58p = 98p$

```
  T  O
  4  0
+ 5  8
  9  8
```

A cup of tea and a teacake cost 98p altogether.

> I will use what I know about the difference between the two plates to work out the cost of an egg.

b) There is one more egg on one plate.

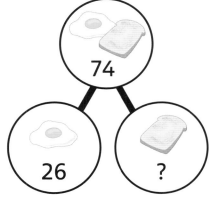

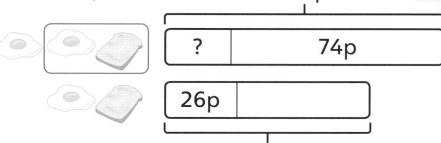

$100p - 74p = 26p$

So one  = 26p.

> I can use a part-whole model to work out the price of the toast.

$74p - 26p = 48p$

One piece of toast costs 48p.

Think together

1 How much more does a teacake cost than an egg?

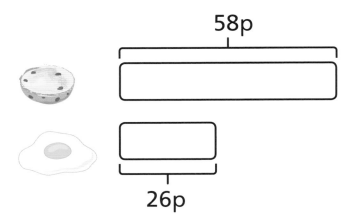

58p

26p

Cup of tea: 40p

Teacake: 58p

Egg: 26p

Toast: 48p

58p ◯ 26p = ⬚ p

A teacake costs ⬚ p more than an egg.

2 Filip buys a cup of tea and an egg.

Filip pays with

How much change does he get?

70p		
40p	26p	?

Filip gets ⬚ p change.

66

3 Josh has some blocks.

He uses them to make these.

CHALLENGE

This is 85 cm long.

This is 55 cm long.

How long is each block?

 = ☐ cm   ☐ = ☐ cm

I think this might be like the egg and toast question from earlier.

67

Solving problems – multiplication and division

Discover

Sale
£5 each

1 **a)** Erik buys four . What is the total cost?

b) Six  cost £12.

How much do three  cost?

Share

a)

> I am going to draw a bar model for this.

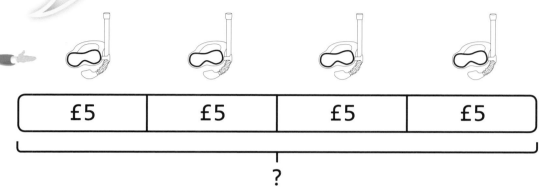

$£5 × 4 = £20$

The total cost is £20.

b) Work out the cost of one beach ball.

$£12 ÷ 6 = £2$

Each 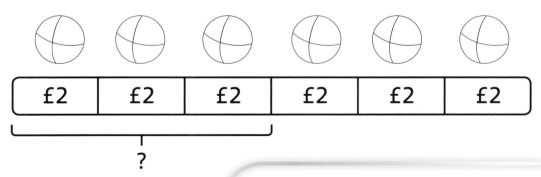 costs £2.

$£2 × 3 = £6$

Three ⊕ cost £6.

> I know that the cost of three ⊕ is half of the cost of six ⊕, so I halved £12.

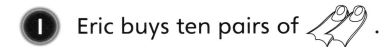

Think together

1 Eric buys ten pairs of 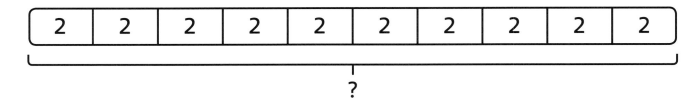 .

How many are there altogether?

| 2 | 2 | 2 | 2 | 2 | 2 | 2 | 2 | 2 | 2 |

?

10 ◯ 2 = ☐

There are ☐ altogether.

2 5 pairs of sunglasses cost £30.

How much does one pair of sunglasses cost?

| ? | |

30

☐ ◯ ☐ = ☐

One pair of sunglasses costs ☐ .

3 Shay and Amy buy these items.

They share them equally.

How many do they each get?

I will draw them and share them out one by one.

I do not think you need to share them one by one. I think there is a quicker way.

71

→ Practice book 2C p50

Solving problems using the four operations

Discover

1 **a)** How many apples are there altogether in bags and boxes?

b) Emily has 25 apples to put into boxes.

Each box can hold five apples. Three boxes are filled.

How many apples are left?

Share

a) There are six bags of two apples.

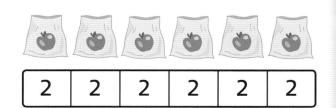

$6 \times 2 = 12$ apples

There are two boxes of five apples.

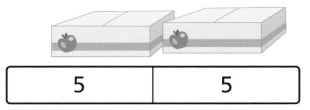

$2 \times 5 = 10$ apples

$12 + 10 = 22$ apples

There are **22** apples altogether.

	T	O
	1	2
+	1	0
	2	2

b) Work out how many apples Emily has packed and then subtract this from the total number of apples to find the difference.

$3 \times 5 = 15$ apples

$25 - 15 = 10$

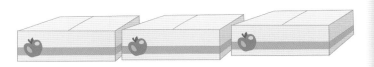

25			
5	5	5	

I can show this on a bar model.

$25 - 5 - 5 - 5 = 10$

There are **10** apples left.

Think together

1

How much does the rice cost in total?

10	10	10

2	2	2	2

$\boxed{} \times \boxed{} = \boxed{}$

$\boxed{} \times \boxed{} = \boxed{}$

$\boxed{} + \boxed{} = \boxed{}$

The total cost of the rice is £ $\boxed{}$.

2 Mantas has 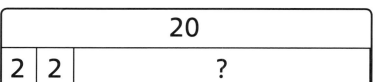 .

How much money does he have left after buying two small bags of rice?

$\boxed{} \times \boxed{} = \boxed{}$

$20 - \boxed{} = \boxed{}$

Mantas has £ $\boxed{}$ left.

20		
2	2	?

CHALLENGE

3 Liam has  .

He buys these bags of rice.

Rice £10 per bag

Rice £10 per bag

How many small bags of rice can he buy with the change?

I am going to draw a bar model to help me with this.

I think there are three different calculations that I need to do.

75

End of unit check

Your teacher will ask you these questions.

1 Adam is saving for a new game.

Adam saved £40 in January.

He saved £30 in February.

How much more money does he need to save?

A £70   **B** £10   **C** £30   **D** £60

2 Which pair of numbers **cannot** go in the boxes to make the calculation correct.

$$1\boxed{} + \boxed{} = 23$$

A 10 and 13   **B** 5 and 8   **C** 8 and 5   **D** 3 and 10

3 Paul has a rope that is 50 m long.

He cuts it into two equal parts.

Which calculation shows the length of each piece?

A 50 + 2 =   **B** 50 − 2 =   **C** 50 × 2 =   **D** 50 ÷ 2 =

4 Hanna has 60 grapes.

She gives 32 to Scott. She gives 15 to Amir.

How many grapes does Hanna have left?

A 13   **B** 47   **C** 28   **D** 17

Think!

Explain the steps you need to solve this question.

Oranges are packed into boxes of four.

I have ten boxes of oranges.

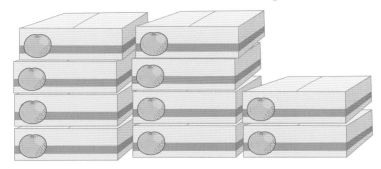

The oranges are put into bags of five.

How many bags of five oranges do I have?

First I _____ .

Then I _____ .

I got the answer _____ .

77

→ **Practice book 2C p56**

Unit 13
Time

In this unit we will ...
⚡ Tell the time to the hour, the half hour and quarter hour
⚡ Tell the time to five minutes
⚡ Find start and end times
⚡ Find out how long something lasts
⚡ Compare amounts of time

Do you remember which is the hour hand and which is the minute hand?

We will need some maths words. Have you heard any of these before?

o'clock   half past

quarter past   quarter to

minute hand   hour hand

duration

We can count forwards or backwards on a number line to help us solve time problems. How many minutes between five minutes past 1 and twenty-five minutes past 1?

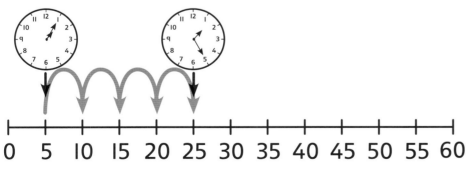

Telling and writing time to the hour and the half hour

Discover

1 **a)** What times do the trips leave?

   b) What time do you think the last clock will show?

Share

a)

o'clock   half past

When the **minute hand** points to 12 it is an **o'clock** time. When it points to 6 it is a **half past** time.

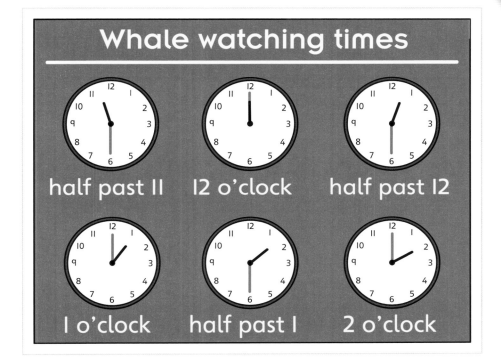

Whale watching times

half past 11   12 o'clock   half past 12

1 o'clock   half past 1   2 o'clock

b) The next half-past time after 2 o'clock looks like this.

The last clock will show half past 2.

Think together

1 What time is it?

> I remembered to look at the **hour hand** and the minute hand.

The time is ☐ o'clock.

2 What time is it?

The time is _____ .

3 **a)** Which circle would you sort each clock into?

CHALLENGE

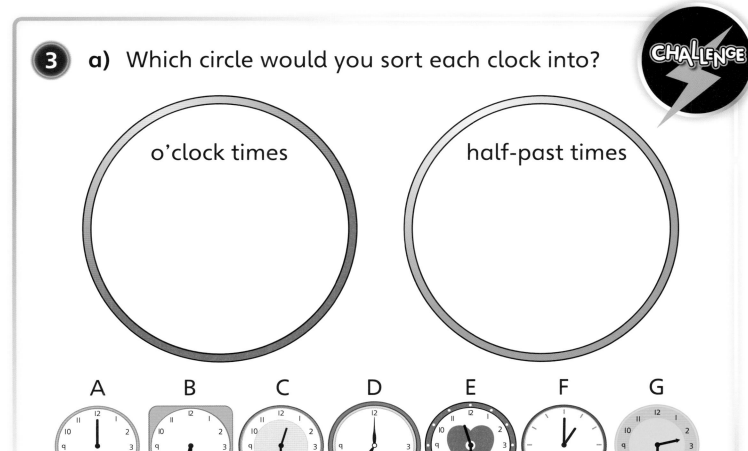

o'clock times

half-past times

A   B   C   D   E   F   G

Did you notice where the minute hand was each time?

b) Where does the minute hand point for o'clock times?

c) Where does the minute hand point for half-past times?

83

Telling time to the quarter hour

Discover

1. **a)** What time will the  be fed?

   b) What time will the be fed?

Share

a)

What if the minute hand travels a quarter of the way around the clock?

We call it **quarter past**. When there is quarter of an hour to go until the next o'clock we call it **quarter to**.

o'clock    quarter past    half past    quarter to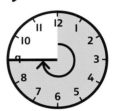

The  will be fed at quarter past 5.

b) The  will be fed at quarter to 6.

Think together

1 **a)** What time does the reptile house open?

The reptile house opens at

_____ .

b) What time does it close?

The reptile house closes at

_____ .

Reptile house

Open   Closed

I will work out what the minute hand says first.

2 What times can you meet the macaws?

You can meet the macaws at

_____ and

_____ .

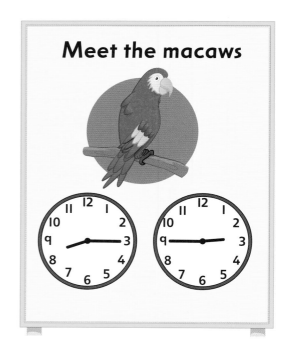

Meet the macaws

3

CHALLENGE

Anna

Kat

Eshan

Kat is going to make quarter past 5.

Eshan is going to make quarter to 1.

Make or draw your own quarter-past and quarter-to times.

Can you read your friend's time?

Where do the hands point for quarter-past times? Where do they point for quarter-to times?

→ Practice book 2C p61

Telling time to 5 minutes

Discover

1 **a)** The bus is due to arrive in 5 minutes.

What time will the bus arrive?

b) What time will the bus arrive if it is 15 minutes late?

Share

a)

Each number on the clock represents another 5 minutes.

Before a half-past time, we can count in 5s to see how many minutes have gone past the o'clock time.

After a half-past time, we can count in 5s to see how many minutes there are to the next o'clock time.

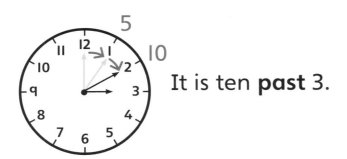

It is ten **past** 3.

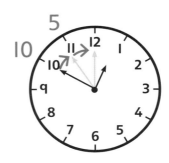

It is ten **to** 1.

Count in 5s to find the answer.

The time now is twenty minutes past 1.

In another 5 minutes the time will be:

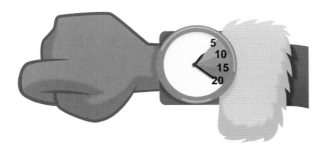

The bus will arrive at twenty-five minutes past 1.

b) The bus was due at twenty-five minutes past 1.

Count on 15 minutes.   Then work out the new time.

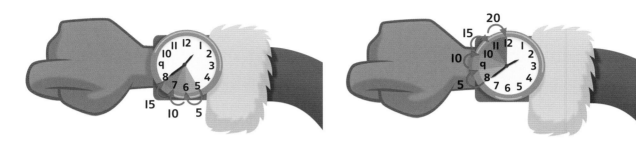

The bus is now due at twenty minutes to 2.

Think together

1 What time is it?

a)

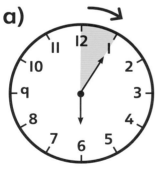

c)

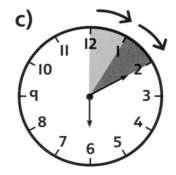

These times are something "past 6".

b)

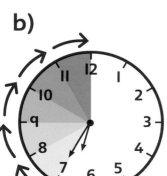

d)

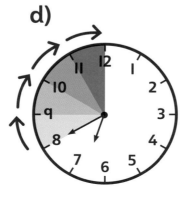

These times are something "to 7".

2 What time is it?

a)

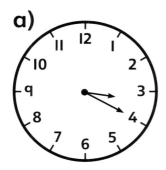

c)

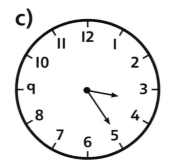

b)

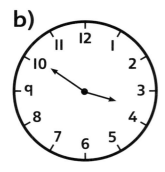

d)

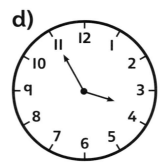

3 How many clock times can you show between 8 o'clock and 9 o'clock?

CHALLENGE

I wonder if you can show some 'past' and some 'to' times?

91

Minutes in an hour

Discover

1 **a)** Malik also ran the race.

He took 80 minutes.

How many hours and minutes did he take?

b) Who took longer out of Eva and Anya?

Share

a)

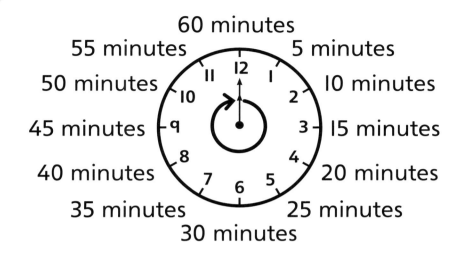

60 minutes
55 minutes   5 minutes
50 minutes   10 minutes
45 minutes   15 minutes
40 minutes   20 minutes
35 minutes   25 minutes
30 minutes

There are 60 minutes in 1 hour.

I will use this to help find the time Malik took in hours and minutes.

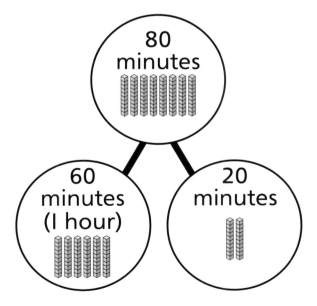

80 minutes

60 minutes (1 hour)   20 minutes

80	
60	20

80 minutes is the same as 1 hour and 20 minutes.

Malik took 1 hour and 20 minutes.

b) Anya took 55 minutes. Eva took 1 hour 10 minutes.

It is easier to compare measurements if they both have the same units.

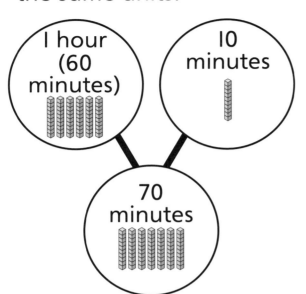

70	
60	10

1 hour and 10 minutes is the same as 70 minutes.

Anya took 55 minutes.
Eva took 70 minutes.

Eva took longer.

Think together

1 **a)**

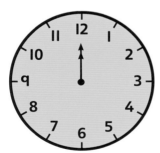

I hour is the same as ☐ minutes.

b)

I hour and 5 minutes is the same as ☐ minutes.

2

[ ] hour and [ ] minutes is the same as [ ] minutes.

3 What is 95 minutes written in hours and minutes?

There are 60 minutes in 1 hour. I need to work out how many more minutes are left.

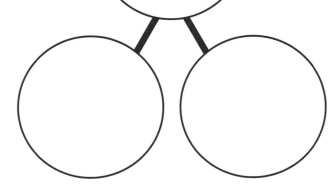

95 minutes is the same as [ ] hour and [ ] minutes.

95

Finding durations of time

Discover

I **a)** They began their journey at five past 4.

How long have they been travelling for so far?

b) How long is left of the journey?

Share

a)

start   time now   10 minutes

The **duration** of something is the amount of time it takes.

I looked at how the minute hand moved from the start to the end. I counted in 5s to find out how many minutes had passed.

I used a number line! I started at the number 5 and counted in 5s to 15.

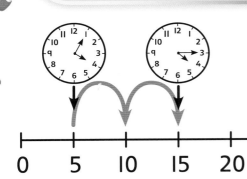

0   5   10   15   20   25   30   35   40   45   50   55   60

They have been travelling for 10 minutes so far.

b) Count from **15** (which is quarter past) until you get to **60** (which is o'clock).

time now   end   45 minutes

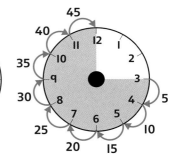

There are 45 minutes left of the journey.

Think together

1 It takes Grandad from ten past 3 until 4 o'clock to mow his lawn.

How long does Grandad take?

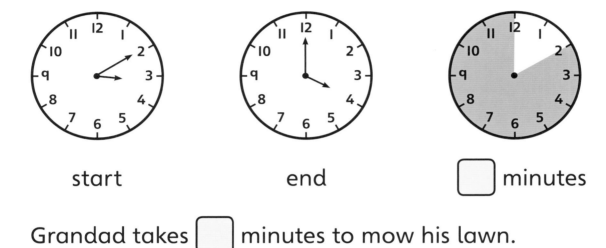

start   end   ☐ minutes

Grandad takes ☐ minutes to mow his lawn.

2 Gran starts gardening at quarter past 3.

She stops at 4 o'clock.

How long does she spend gardening?

start   end   ☐ minutes

Gran spends ☐ minutes gardening.

3 Gran plays a board game from five past 6 until twenty-five to 7.

How long does she play for?

To work out this answer, I need to count in 5s from 5 up to 35.

That's not right! The number you need to count to is 25.

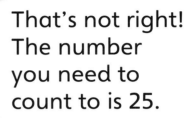

Who is right?

Why do you think this?

Gran plays for ☐ minutes.

99

Comparing durations of time

Discover

1 **a)** Look at the timetable above.

Which of these journeys takes the longest?

Garforth to Hyde Park

Hyde Park to Whinmoor

b) How long does it take to go from Garforth to Whinmoor?

Share

I can look at the start time and the end time and see how many minutes have gone by.

a) Garforth ⟶ Hyde Park

five past 11 ⟶ twenty-five to 12

  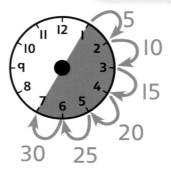

   start   end   30 minutes

Garforth to Hyde Park takes 30 minutes.

Hyde Park   ⟶ Whinmoor

twenty-five to 12 ⟶ 12 o'clock

  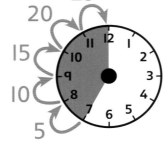

   start   end   25 minutes

I can compare the durations using a number line.

Hyde Park to Whinmoor takes 25 minutes.

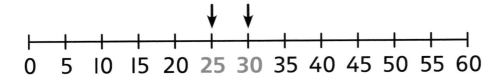

Garforth to Hyde Park takes the longest.

b) Garforth ⟶ Whinmoor

five past 11 ⟶ 12 o'clock

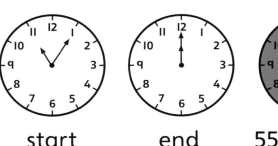

start   end   55 minutes

It takes 55 minutes to go from Garforth to Whinmoor.

Another way is to add the two journey times you already worked out.

Think together

1

Start: 3 o'clock
End: 6 o'clock

Start: 5 o'clock
End: 7 o'clock

Which journey takes longer?

 takes ⬜ hours.

 takes ⬜ hours.

⬜ hours are more than ⬜ hours.

The _____ journey takes longer.

2

I hour 30 minutes

I hour 25 minutes

Which journey takes longer?

☐ hour and ☐ minutes is more than ☐ hour and

☐ minutes, so the _____ journey takes longer.

3

 Shaan

 Maya

 CHALLENGE

Race

Race

I hour I5 minutes

70 minutes

Who ran faster?

I will work out how many hours are in Maya's time first, to help compare them. It will be easier to compare the times if they have the same units.

_____ is less time than _____ ,

so _____ ran faster.

103

Finding the end time

Discover

1 a) What time does the dough need to go in the oven?

b) The bread needs to bake for 30 minutes. What time should it be taken out of the oven?

Share

a)

> Can I find the end time by counting forwards?

time now   time taken   end time

The dough needs to go in the oven at twenty-five minutes past 1.

b)

> I used a number line to find the baking time.

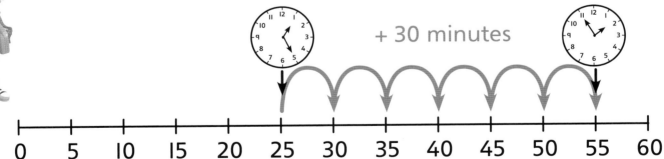

+ 30 minutes

| | | | | | | | | | | | | |
|0|5|10|15|20|25|30|35|40|45|50|55|60|

The bread should be taken out of the oven at fifty-five minutes past 1. We call this time five minutes to 2.

Think together

1 It is twenty-five minutes past 6.

A pizza takes 20 minutes to cook. What time will it be ready?

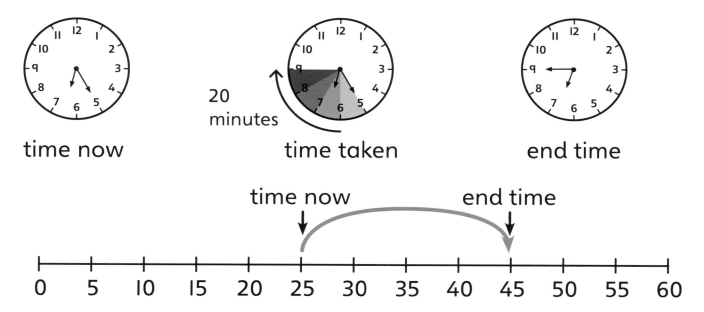

time now   20 minutes   time taken   end time

The pizza will be ready at _____ .

2 It is twenty-five minutes past 7.

These 🍪 take 25 minutes to cook. What time will they be ready?

time now   25 minutes   time taken   end time

The 🍪 will be ready at _____ .

3 The Kids Cookery Show lasts for 15 minutes.

It starts at twenty-five minutes to 8.

What time does it finish?

CHALLENGE

Lucy

I started on 25 and counted three jumps of 5 to show 15 minutes. I ended on 40. The answer is 40 minutes past 8.

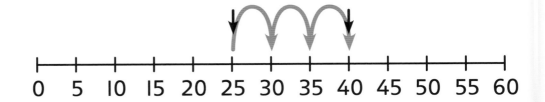

0 5 10 15 20 25 30 35 40 45 50 55 60

Filip

I started on 35 because twenty-five to 8 is the same as thirty-five past 7. I counted 15 minutes and ended on 50. The answer is fifty minutes past 7 which we say as ten to 8.

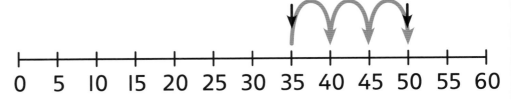

0 5 10 15 20 25 30 35 40 45 50 55 60

Who is right?

I can use my knowledge of 'past' and 'to' to help me.

107

Finding the start time

Discover

1. a) What time did the match start?

   b) Can you find the same answer using a number line?

Share

a) We found the end time by counting forwards. I wonder if we can find the start time by counting backwards?

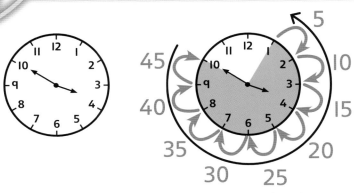

time now   time taken   start time

The match started at five minutes past 3.

b) Think about whether you need to count forwards or backwards on a number line.

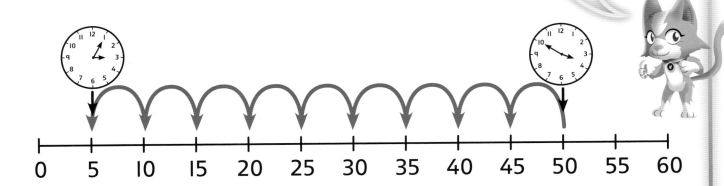

If we start at the number 50 and count back 45 we end on the number 5.

The match started at five minutes past 3.

Think together

1 Assembly started 15 minutes ago.

What time did it start?

time now

time taken

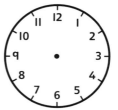

start time

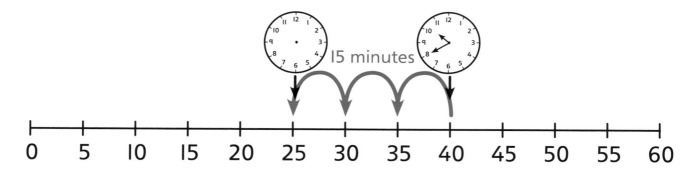

15 minutes

| 0 | 5 | 10 | 15 | 20 | 25 | 30 | 35 | 40 | 45 | 50 | 55 | 60 |

2 Playtime started 20 minutes ago.

What time did it start?

time now

time taken

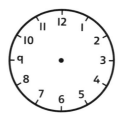

start time

CHALLENGE

3 A maths test takes 30 minutes.

Tim and Janet finished at different times.

I finished at quarter to 12.

I finished at five minutes to 12.

What time did they each start?

Who started first?

I will use a number line to help me.

Hours in a day

Discover

Next day

Is it safe to drink?

1 **a)** How many times in a day does the hour hand go around the clock?

How many hours are there in one day?

b) Should Sunil drink the smoothie? Why?

Share

a)

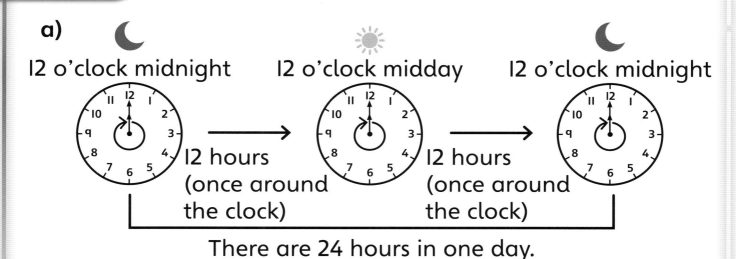

12 o'clock midnight

12 o'clock midday

12 o'clock midnight

12 hours (once around the clock)

12 hours (once around the clock)

There are **24** hours in one day.

The hour hand goes around the clock twice in one day.

b) Look at the time Sunil wants to drink the smoothie.

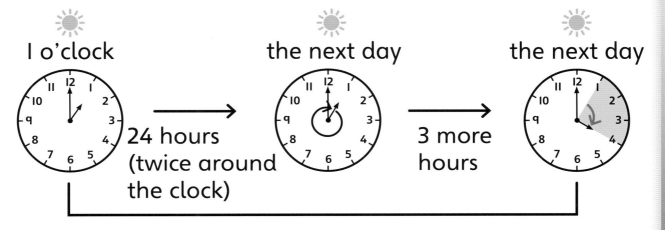

I o'clock

the next day

the next day

24 hours (twice around the clock)

3 more hours

4 o'clock is **more than** 24 hours later.

Sunil should not drink the smoothie as it is not safe to drink.

It should have been used by I o'clock in the daytime the next day.

Think together

1 Today is Tuesday. When will the postman be back?

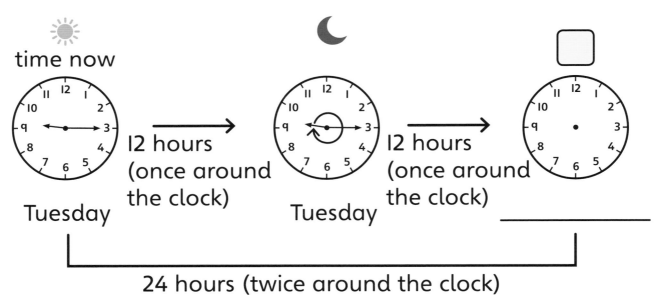

time now

12 hours (once around the clock)

Tuesday

12 hours (once around the clock)

Tuesday

_____

24 hours (twice around the clock)

The postman will be back on _____

at the time of _____ .

2

Take the bandage off in 24 hours.

It is quarter past I on Tuesday. Can I take the bandage off?

24 hours after twenty-five past I on Monday, the time will be _____ and the day will be _____ .

She _____ take the bandage off now.

3 An explorer wants to climb a mountain in 24 hours.

Here are the times when he started and finished his climb.

CHALLENGE

start time

end time

I don't think we can answer this question. We need more information.

Did he climb the mountain in time?

What else do you need to know to answer the question?

115

→ Practice book 2C p82

End of unit check

Your teacher will ask you these questions.

1 PE is at five minutes to 2.

What will the clock look like?

A 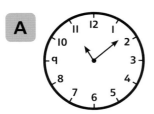 B 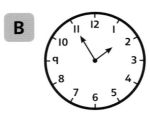 C 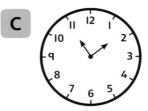 D

2 Children were timed solving a maze.

Alex	Olivia	Ella
I hour and 20 minutes	85 minutes	I hour and 30 minutes

Who left the maze first?

A Alex

B Olivia

C Ella

D Olivia and Ella left together

3 🚌 arrives at ten minutes past 4.

🚌 arrives 25 minutes later.

What time does 🚌 arrive?

A twenty-five minutes past 4

B twenty-five minutes to 5

C quarter to 4

D quarter to 5

4 Music starts at quarter past I. It ends at ten minutes to 2.

Art starts at twenty-five minutes past 2 and ends at 3 o'clock.

Which is longer?

A The art lesson is longer.   **C** They are the same.

B The music lesson is longer.

5 A car is parked on Thursday morning at this time.

It can stay for 24 hours. When does it have to move?

A On Friday at ten minutes to II in the night.

B On Thursday at ten minutes to II in the night.

C On Friday at ten minutes past II in the day.

D On Friday at ten minutes to II in the day.

Think!

The answers to these times have been given to you.

Explain how you know whether they are right.

twenty-five minutes
past 6

twenty minutes
to 3

These words
might help you.

hour hand

minute hand

117

→ Practice book 2C p85

Unit 14
Weight, volume and temperature

In this unit we will ...
- ⚡ Compare and measure mass
- ⚡ Compare and measure volume
- ⚡ Measure temperature
- ⚡ Read a thermometer

We will use < and > to compare. Which would you use to complete this sentence?

Watermelon ◯ apple

We will need some maths words.
Which of these have you heard before?

mass　　　**balance**　　　**weighing scales**

grams, g　　　　**kilograms, kg**

litres, l　　**millilitres, ml**　　**volume**　　**capacity**

temperature　　　**thermometer**

degrees Celsius, °C　　　**estimate**

approximation

We will use different things to
measure. Have you used any of
these? Can you match the names?

thermometer

balance scale

measuring jug

weighing scale

Comparing mass

Discover

1 **a)** How can you find out what each person should carry?

b) 1 ⊚ has the same **mass** as 2 🍶.

What is the mass of 3 ⊚ in bottles?

Share

You should use a balance to be exact when comparing mass.

a)

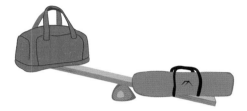

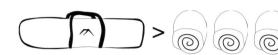

We know the heaviest, but we don't know which is **lightest** yet.

I remember that we can use > to mean **heavier than**, and < to mean **lighter than**.

b)

3 have the same mass as 3 lots of 2 , which is 6 .

Think together

1 Put the torch, mallet and tent in order of mass.

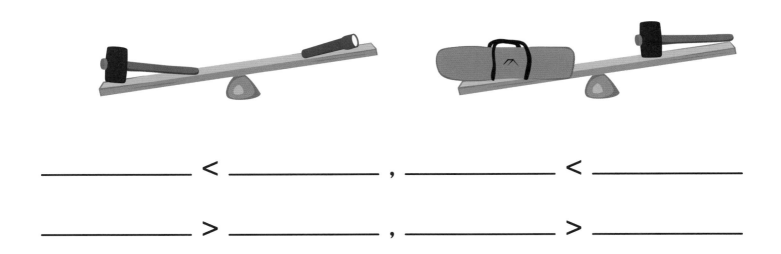

_____ < _____ , _____ < _____

_____ > _____ , _____ > _____

2

The has the same mass as 10 🍼 .

Write the mass of the other items in 🍼 .

a)

b)

3 Another family go camping.

Molly says, 'My bag is twice as heavy as a tent.'

Jack says, 'My bag is half as heavy as Molly's.'

Dad says, 'My bag is five times as heavy as Molly's.'

a) Whose bag is heaviest?

_____'s bag is heaviest.

b) Whose bag is lightest?

_____'s bag is lightest.

I wonder how many tents balance each bag.

123

Measuring mass in grams ❶

Discover

Salt dough

You need:

100 g flour
50 g salt
spoonful of oil
water

Instructions:
1) Measure the mass of the flour and the salt carefully.
2) Mix with a spoonful of oil.
3) Add water gradually and mix.

❶ **a)** How can the children measure the flour and the salt accurately?

b) How much flour is this?

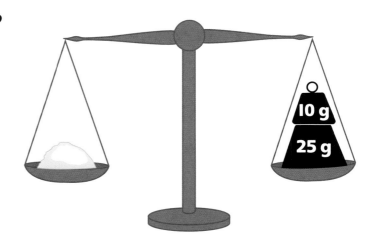

Share

a) 100 g means 100 **grams**.

A gram is a unit for measuring mass.

We measure mass accurately by weighing.

I know to put  on the balance and to add flour carefully until both sides are balanced.

I will balance  to measure the salt. If the salt becomes too heavy, I will take some away.

b)

10 + 25 = 35

10 g + 25 g = 35 g

The mass of the flour is 35 g.

I can use ▢▢▢▢▢▢▢▢▢ ▢ to help.

125

Think together

1 How could you use these weights to measure the flour and the salt?

You need:
60 g flour
30 g salt

60 g flour   **30 g salt**

Copy and complete the sentences.

☐ + ☐ balances the flour.   ☐ + ☐ balances the salt.

2 Marta wants to measure her salt dough models.

She adds weights until they balance.

The mass of the ☆ is twice the mass of the ♡.

Copy and complete the sentences.

The ♡ has a mass of ☐ g.

The ☆ has a mass of ☐ g.

3 You can also measure using weighing scales.

The arrow points at the total mass.

Copy and complete the sentences about the salt dough models.

The has a mass of ☐ g.

The  has a mass of ☐ g.

→ Practice book 2C p90

Measuring mass in grams 2

Discover

1 **a)** What is the mass of each 🐹 ?

b) Another 🐹 weighs more than the smallest 🐹
but less than the middle 🐹 .
What could its mass be?

Share

a) The vet's scales count in **hundreds**.

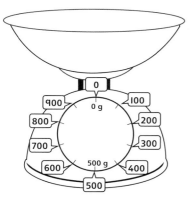

I used a number line to work out which numbers are missing from the scale.

0   500

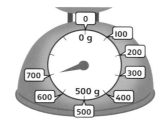

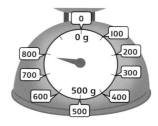

The smallest has a mass of 300 g.

The middle has a mass of 700 g.

The largest has a mass of just under 800 g.

We can say it is 800 g to the nearest 100 g.

b)

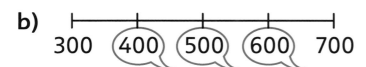

300   400   500   600   700

The other could have a mass of more than 300 g

and less than 700 g.

Think together

1 Read the scales for these pets.

Write the mass of each pet to the nearest 100 g.

a)

0
100
0 g
200
300
500 g
?

☐ g

b)

0 g
500 g

☐ g

2 The vet weighs some hamsters, a squirrel and a rat.

a) Copy and complete the statements.

The _____ is the lightest.

The _____ is the heaviest.

b) Order the animals by mass.

lightest _____ heaviest.

3 Hold a in your hands (carefully!).

Find some objects in the classroom. Hold the in one hand and an object in the other.

Estimate whether they have a mass of more than 100 g or less than 100 g.

Write your results in a diagram like this.

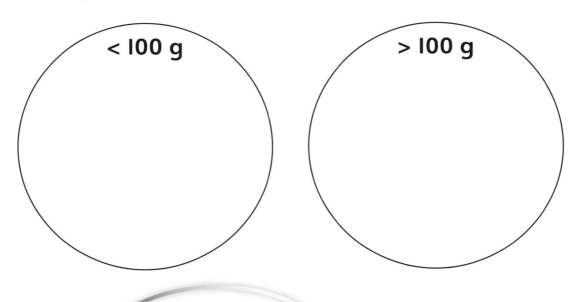

< 100 g

> 100 g

I think that a ruler feels lighter than 100 g.

Then check your predictions using balance scales.

131

→ **Practice book 2C p93**

Measuring mass in kilograms

Discover

1 Anya is buying 🍍. Milo is buying 🍎.

a) Who will need a stronger bag?

b) What is the mass of the 🍌 ?

Share

a) A **kilogram** is a heavier unit than grams for measuring mass.

'Kilo' is short for kilogram.

Try holding in your hands.

It is quite heavy. Don't drop it!

I will read the scales.

The 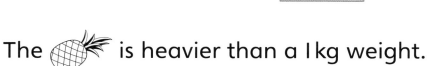 is heavier than a 1 kg weight.

The 🍎 are less than 1 kg on the dial.

Anya will need a stronger bag.

b) This scale measures in kilograms.

The mass of the 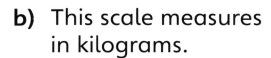 is 2 kilograms.

You can write 2 kg. Some people say '2 kilos'.

133

Think together

1

Write the mass of each item in kilograms.

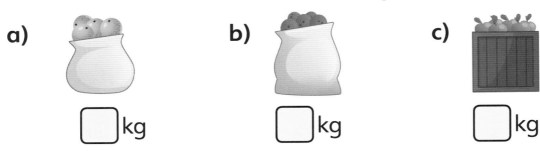

a) ◻ kg

b) ◻ kg

c) ◻ kg

2 Mr Green has three crates.

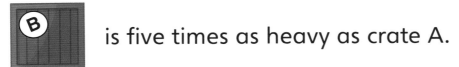 is five times as heavy as crate A.

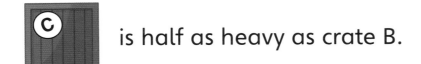 is half as heavy as crate B.

What is the mass of each crate?

0 kg   10 kg   20 kg   30 kg   40 kg   50 kg

Crate A ◻ kg   Crate B ◻ kg   Crate C ◻ kg

3 How many grams is the same mass as I kg?

I will work out how many there are in 5 .

135

Comparing volume

Discover

1 **a)** How can you find out which cone holds more popcorn?

b) How can you find out which glass has the larger capacity?

Share

a)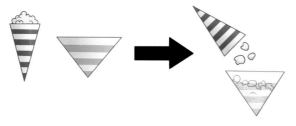

I will pour the popcorn from one cone into the other cone.

The red cone does not fill the blue cone.

 holds less.

red cone < blue cone

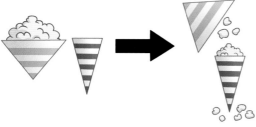

The blue cone fills the red cone and more is left.

 holds more.

blue cone > red cone

I will pour the popcorn from both cones into identical containers.

half full   three-quarters full

The blue cone holds more popcorn.

b)

I will use spoons of rice to measure the capacity.

Volume is the amount of space something takes up. Capacity is the maximum volume a container can hold.

The tall glass holds 10 spoonfuls.

The short glass holds 5 spoonfuls.

The tall glass has the larger capacity.

× 10

× 5

Think together

1 Meg pours the tea from 3  into identical jugs.

A   B   C

a) Which  had the least tea in it?

b) Which had the most tea in it?

c) Choose the correct word to complete the sentence.

a quarter	half	three-quarters

The jug for C is _____ full.

2 The capacity of the is 10 spoonfuls of rice.

The holds half as much as the .

The  holds five times as much as the .

× 10

What is the capacity of each container in spoonfuls?

a)

b)

3

a) How many 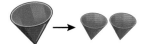 does the big cone hold?

b) How many  does the bucket hold?

I will count in 5s.

CHALLENGE

139

→ Practice book 2C p99

Measuring volume in millilitres ❶

Discover

We need to measure vinegar for our volcano experiment.

Tariq

Anya

I teaspoon holds 5 ml.

Vinegar 100 ml

5 ml vinegar

10 ml vinegar

15 ml vinegar

20 ml vinegar

100 ml vinegar

❶ **a)** How can Tariq and Anya measure each amount of vinegar accurately?

b) Tariq put 30 ml of vinegar in a pot.

How many teaspoons is that?

Share

Millilitres are units for measuring volume.

I teaspoon holds 5 ml.

 'ml' stands for millilitres.

a)

| 5 ml vinegar | 10 ml vinegar | 15 ml vinegar | 20 ml vinegar |

 5 ml  5 ml  5 ml  5 ml

10 ml  10 ml  10 ml

 15 ml  15 ml

 20 ml

I will count in 5s.

100 ml would be lots of teaspoons. I will use a measuring jug.

Tariq and Anya can measure the vinegar accurately using a teaspoon or a measuring jug.

b)

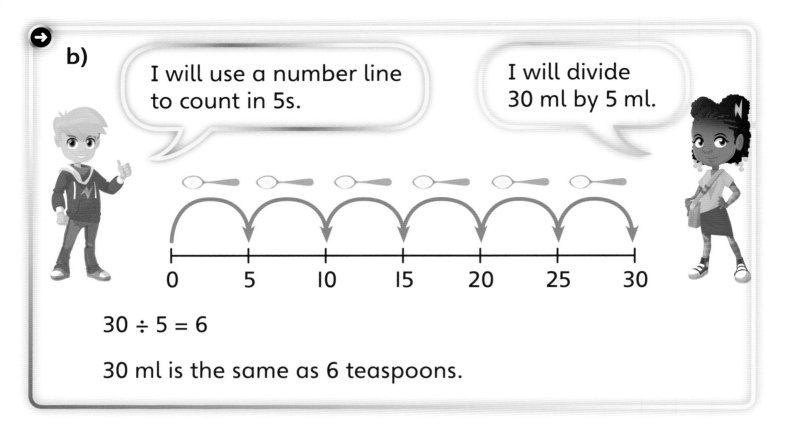

I will use a number line to count in 5s.

I will divide 30 ml by 5 ml.

$30 \div 5 = 6$

30 ml is the same as 6 teaspoons.

Think together

1 Write the volume of vinegar in each jug in millilitres.

a)

[ ] ml

b)

[ ] ml

2 Anya used teaspoons to put vinegar into these jugs.

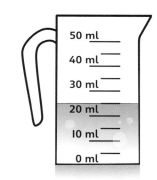
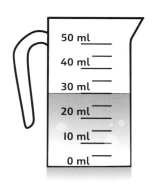

a) How many millilitres of vinegar did Anya put into the jugs altogether?

Anya put ☐ ml of vinegar into the jugs.

b) How many teaspoons is that?

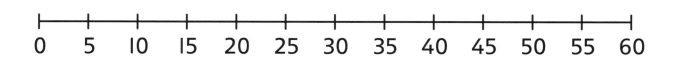

☐ ml ÷ 5 = ☐ teaspoons.

3 What volume of vinegar is in the jug?

CHALLENGE

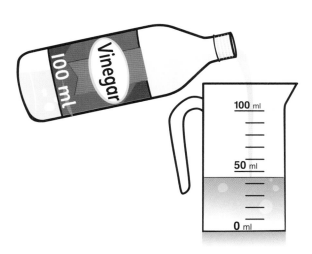

The level is halfway between 40 ml and 50 ml.

143

Measuring volume in millilitres **2**

Discover

1 **a)** How much pasta sauce has Jack made?

b) Will it all fit in one  ?

Share

a)

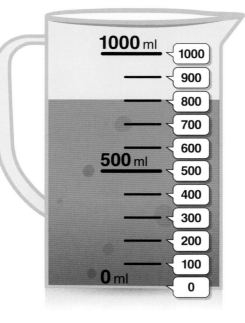

We can count in 100s, like we did with grams.

The level is at 800 ml.

Jack has made 800 ml of pasta sauce.

b)

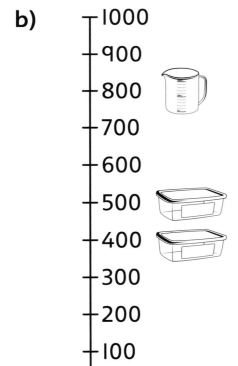

800 is greater than 500 and 400.

There is too much sauce to fit in one .

It will fit in two .

Think together

1 What is the volume of orange juice in each jug in millilitres?

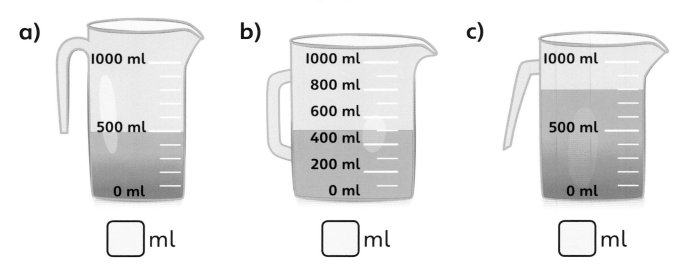

a) ☐ ml

b) ☐ ml

c) ☐ ml

2 Jack needs more than 300 ml of milk but less than 500 ml.

Which jug should he use?

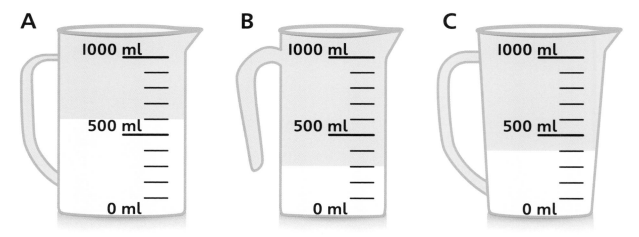

A   B   C

Use a number line to help you.

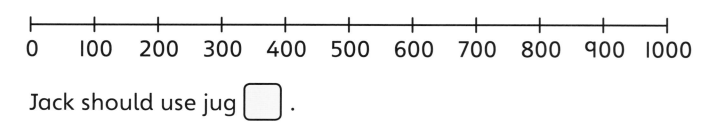

0 100 200 300 400 500 600 700 800 900 1000

Jack should use jug ☐ .

146

3 This does not reach an exact 100 ml line.

What is a good approximation?

a)

Approximation means an answer that is close but does not have to be exact.

We need to think about which hundred it is nearest to.

b) Write an approximation for each of these volumes.

Approximately ☐ ml.   Approximately ☐ ml.

147

→ Practice book 2C p105

Measuring volume in litres

Discover

1 **a)** How many large  can Kat fill from the  ?

b) Kat uses 1 full large  and 1 full small  .

How much is left in the  ?

Share

A **litre** is a larger unit for measuring volume.

A litre is the same volume as 1000 ml.

One litre is the same as 10 ×

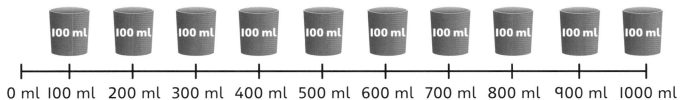

'5 l' is short for 5 litres.

a) The large 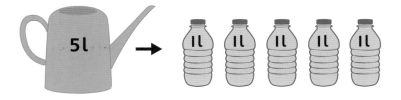 holds 5 litres.

I will count in 5s.

 5l   5l

5l 5l   10 l

5l 5l 5l   15 l

5l 5l 5l 5l   20 l   4 × 5 = 20

I can solve this with a division.

The ☐ holds 20 litres.

Kat can fill 4 large 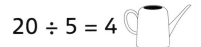 from the ☐.

20 ÷ 5 = 4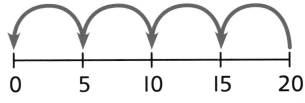

149

b) Kat uses 5 l and 2 l altogether.

$$5 \quad + \quad 2 \quad = 7$$

She uses 7 l of water.

20 – 7 = 13

There are 13 litres left in the ⬜.

Think together

1 Kat waters 3 flowers for 5 days. She gives a flower the same amount of water each day.

Complete the table with the amounts of water.

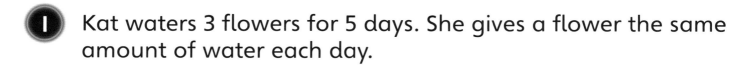

	Mon	Tues	Weds	Thurs	Fri	Total
🌻	5 l	5 l	5 l	5 l	5 l	
🌱						15 l
🌼						5 l

2 Choose a sensible estimate for the volume of each item.

1 l   2 l   5 l   10 l   25 l   40 l   100 l

This is 1 litre.

a)

b)

c)

3 Kat has a 5 l .

Her mum has an 8 l .

a) They want to measure exactly 3 l. How can they do it?

b) They want to measure exactly 2 l. Is it possible?

I think I will pour water from one into the other.

CHALLENGE

151

Measuring temperature using a thermometer

Discover

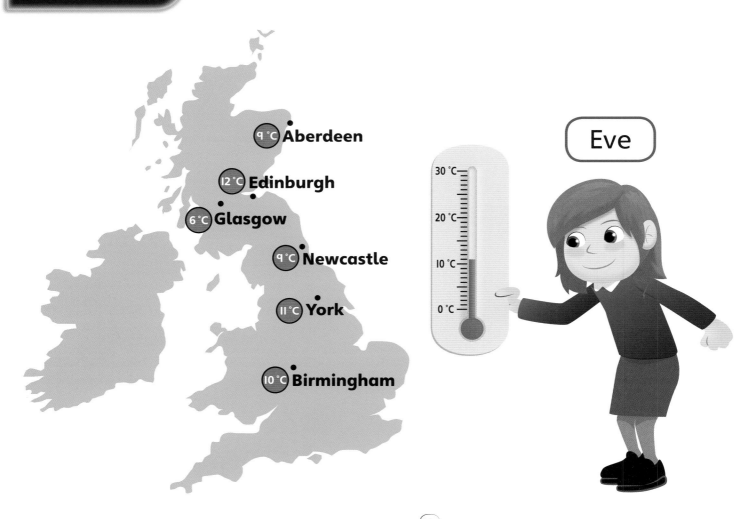

1 a) Eve is at home looking at a 🌡.

   Where does Eve live?

   b) Marta says, 'Where I live is 3 °C warmer than Aberdeen.'

   Where does Marta live?

Share

Celsius is a unit for measuring **temperature**.

'**°C**' stands for '**degrees Celsius**'. You can just say 'degrees'.

a) The **thermometer** scale shows degrees.

This shows 11 °C.

It is 11 °C in York.

Eve lives in York.

I will count on from 10 °C.

b) Look at the map.

It is 9 °C in Aberdeen.

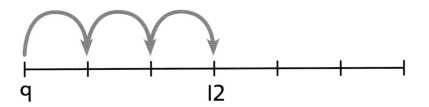

It is 12 °C where Marta lives.

Marta lives in Edinburgh.

The warmer the temperature, the higher the number. I will count on.

Think together

1 What is the temperature shown on each ?

a)

b)

c)

d)

2 Where do these people live?

a) Rav says, "It is 3 degrees cooler than Aberdeen."

b) Sue says, "It is 3 degrees warmer than Bristol."

c) Jon says, "It is warmer than Penzance but cooler than London."

3 Simon lives in Oxford.

He has three .

One is in the sun.

One is in the shade.

One is broken.

Can you work out which is which?

A

0 °C   10 °C   20 °C   30 °C   40 °C   50 °C   60 °C   70 °C   80 °C   90 °C   100 °C

B

0 °C   10 °C   20 °C   30 °C   40 °C   50 °C   60 °C   70 °C   80 °C   90 °C   100 °C

C

0 °C   10 °C   20 °C   30 °C   40 °C   50 °C   60 °C   70 °C   80 °C   90 °C   100 °C

I wonder what a usual summer temperature is in the UK.

155

Reading thermometers

Discover

1 a) What is the temperature of Baby Bear's ?

   b) Whose is hotter, Mummy Bear's or Daddy Bear's?

Share

a) Every line marks 10 degrees.

I will count in 10s.

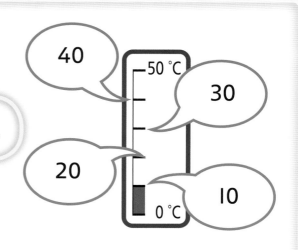

40
30
20
10

Baby Bear's is 10 °C.

Mummy Bear

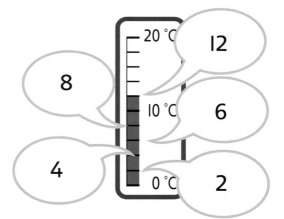

8
12
4
6
2

b) Mummy Bear's counts in 2s.

Mummy Bear's  is 12 °C.

Daddy Bear's counts in 5s.

Daddy Bear's is 15 °C.

Halfway between 10 and 20 is 15.

Daddy Bear

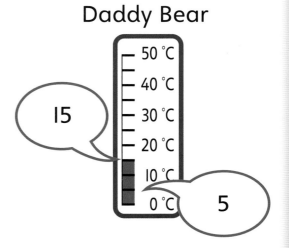

15
5

15 °C > 12 °C

Daddy Bear's is hotter.

Think together

1 Write the temperature shown on each .

a)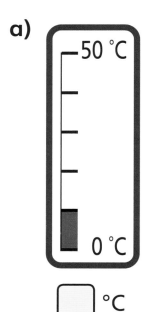

⬜ °C

b)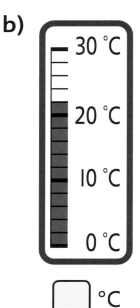

⬜ °C

c)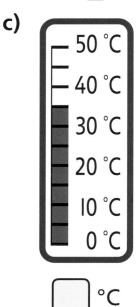

⬜ °C

d)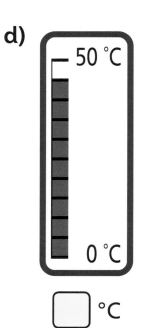

⬜ °C

2 Which 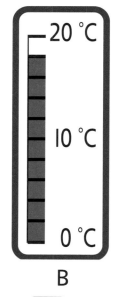 shows the hotter temperature?

a)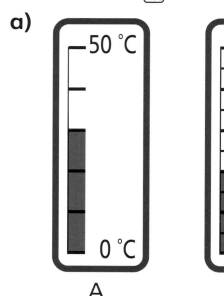

A   B

Thermometer ⬜ shows the hotter temperature.

b)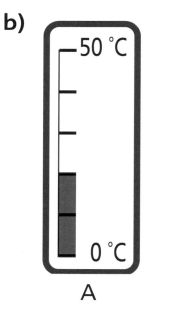

A   B

Thermometer ⬜ shows the hotter temperature.

3 Choose a sensible measurement for each picture.

Let's look carefully at the thermometers.

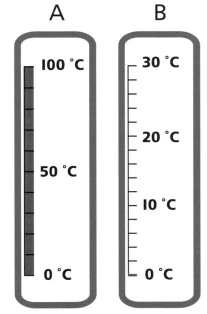

A   B   C   D   E

100 °C	30 °C	100 °C	100 °C	100 °C
50 °C	20 °C	50 °C	50 °C	50 °C
0 °C	10 °C	0 °C	0 °C	0 °C
	0 °C			

159

→ **Practice book 2C p114**

End of unit check

Your teacher will ask you these questions.

1 What is the mass of the 🍎?

A 20 g　　　**B** 25 g　　　**C** 5 g　　　**D** 50 g

2 How many millilitres of juice are now in the ⌣ ?

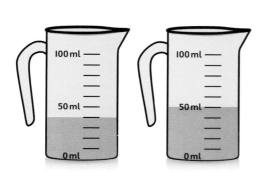 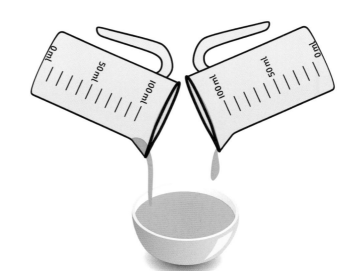

A 40 ml　　　**B** 900 ml　　　**C** 10 ml　　　**D** 90 ml

3 It is 8 degrees warmer inside than outside.

Which  shows inside? Which  shows outside?

A

30 °C
20 °C
10 °C
0 °C

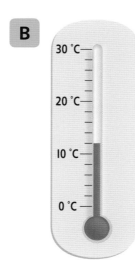

B

30 °C
20 °C
10 °C
0 °C

C

50 °C
0 °C

D

50 °C
0 °C

Think!

Milo balances these ▭.

Work out the mass of each ▭.

A ▭ = ▭ kg   B ▭ = ▭ kg   C ▭ = ▭ kg

161

→ **Practice book 2C p117**

We have learned lots of new things this year!

Yes, we can learn anything if we try hard!

Holiday fun

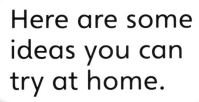

Here are some ideas you can try at home.

Let's dance!

Make up your own dance with 10 steps.

You can move forwards, backwards, left or right.

You can turn clockwise or anticlockwise.

Describe the moves of your dance to a friend and ask them to do it.

Did they do it right?

Minutes and hours

Play this game with a friend.

Take it in turns to say a time.

How many clock times can you say between 2 o'clock and half past 3?

You can play this game on your own too.

How many clock times do you know between 2 o'clock and half past 3?

How many clock times do you know between quarter past 4 and 6 o'clock?

Write them down.

_____

_____

_____

What's the time, Mr Wolf?

Play this game with friends.

- Line up in a row and choose one person to be Mr Wolf.
- Mr Wolf must stand away from everyone with their back turned.
- You must all shout together 'What's the time Mr Wolf?'
- Mr Wolf says a time, such as 2 o'clock. You then all take that number of steps forward.
- You keep asking Mr Wolf the time and taking steps forward.
- When Mr Wolf chooses, he can answer by shouting 'Dinner time!'. Mr Wolf then turns around and tries to catch you! Run away fast!
- Mr Wolf can also say times that are not o'clock times, such as half past 2. However, if you step forward when Mr Wolf doesn't say an o'clock time, you are out!

Making models

You will need an adult to help you with this activity.

Make fun models out of salt dough.
See if you can make models that weigh 50 g, 100 g, 150 g and 200 g. You will need to measure the mass of your models using balance scales.

To make salt dough, you need:

500 g flour

250 g salt

Instructions:

1) Measure the mass of the flour and the salt carefully.
2) Mix with a spoonful of oil.
3) Add water gradually and mix.

I have enjoyed learning new things!

Yes, even when we made mistakes we were learning!

What we have learned

Can you do all these things?

⚡ Describe direction and movement

⚡ Use mental addition and subtraction

⚡ Problem solve with different methods

⚡ Tell the time and compare durations of time

⚡ Measure and compare mass, volume and temperature

Now you are ready to continue your maths journey in Year 3!

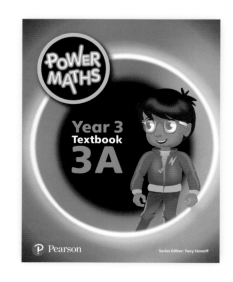

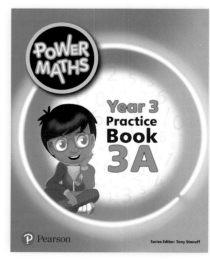